William Wallace: Scotland's Great Freedom Fighter

Celtic Heroes and Legends

History Nerds

Published by History Nerds, 2022.

WILLIAM WALLACE: SCOTLAND'S GREAT FREEDOM FIGHTER

First edition. July 8, 2022.

Copyright © 2022 History Nerds.

ISBN: 979-8215776001

Written by History Nerds.

Also by History Nerds

Ancient Empires
The Ottoman Empire
Rome: The Rise and Fall
The Mongol Empire
The Assyrian Empire
Ancient Egypt

Celtic Heroes and Legends
Celtic History
William Butler Yeats: Nobel Prize Winning Poet
Robert the Bruce
Scáthach
Finn McCool
William Wallace: Scotland's Great Freedom Fighter

Frauen des Krieges
Boudica: Königin der Icener
Jeanne d'Arc

Irena Sendler - Deutsche Ausgabe
Virginia Hall
Königin Amanirenas
Anne Frank
Florence Nightingale
Nakano Takeko
Lyudmila Pawlitschenko
Lagertha

Geschichte der welt
Die Geschichte Schottlands
Die Geschichte von Wales

Great Wars of the World
War Omnibus
World War 1
World War 2
The Napoleonic Wars: One Shot at Glory
The Serbian Revolution: 1804-1835
Peace Won by the Saber: The Crimean War, 1853-1856
The American Civil War

Pirate Chronicles
Grace O'Malley: The Pirate Queen of Ireland
Blackbeard
William Kidd

Ching Shih
Anne Bonny

The History of England
Roman Britain
Medieval England
The Wars of the Roses
Tudor England

The History of the Vikings
The History of the Vikings
Vikings
Longships on Restless Seas

Weltenbrand: Die großen Konflikte
Erster Weltkrieg
Zweiter Weltkrieg
Die Napoleonischen Kriege

Women of War
Women of War Omnibus: Books 1-10
Boudica: Queen of the Iceni
Joan of Arc
Irena Sendler

Virginia Hall
Queen Amanirenas
Anne Frank
Florence Nightingale
Nakano Takeko
Lyudmila Pavlichenko
Lagertha

World History
The History of the United Kingdom
The History of Ireland
The History of America
The History of Scotland
The History of Wales
The History of India
The History of Canada

Standalone
Grace O'Malley: Die Piratenkönigin von Irland

William Wallace
Scotland's Great Freedom Fighter

Introduction

The history of the Scottish nation is full to the brim with glorious heroes and epic struggles. Throughout the centuries of its fight for independence, Scotland gave birth to some truly exceptional men and women, who went above and beyond the call of duty for the freedom of their home country. This fight for independence has ever since inspired every Scottish person - and even bolstered people all across the world. In modern times, the heroic exploits of these fierce men and women have been the subject of numerous movies and TV shows. Arguably the most famous one of these is "Braveheart", the Hollywood portrayal of one of the greatest heroes of Scotland - William Wallace. Who was this great Scottish freedom fighter? Who was this man who willingly laid down his life for the independence of the nation into which he was born? In this book we will try to unravel the life and times of William Wallace, piecing together his puzzled and short life of struggle and war.

Even though the story of William Wallace seems famous and retold many times - as it is - there is still a lot about this hero that we simply do not know. Much that pertains to his youth, origins, and exploits is simply clouded - the rolling wheel of time obscures the historic fact, which was poorly documented in the Scottish Middle Ages. Nevertheless, what we do know is enough to portray a picture of unyielding perseverance, of bravery and a burning desire for freedom - of free will sacrifice for a greater cause. This is the story of one of Scotland's greatest sons: William Wallace.

Chapter I

In our book that was centered on Robert the Bruce, we talked of powerful noble families with kingly ties and deep roots that go back to centuries. When such individuals and families are considered, medieval historians certainly devoted more attention to them, preserving much more information for posterity. Alas, this is not the case with the story of William Wallace, a man whose exact origins are still debated, and about which not much is known. What we do know is that he was born into lesser nobility. The year of his birth is likewise unknown for certain, but scholars agree that he was born sometime around 1270 AD, at a time when Scotland was for a while in relative peace with its larger and powerful neighbor to the south. After the inconclusive Battle of Largs, which the Scots fought against the Kingdom of Norway on October 2nd, 1263, Scotland entered a period of some 40 years of peace and stability. The battle, although inconclusive, is generally viewed as having ended in Scottish favor, as it broke the 500-years-old pressure that the Norwegians and the Vikings in general exerted on Scotland and its isles. Around this time, perhaps some seven years later, William Wallace was supposedly born.

The first piece of the puzzle surrounding the origins of William Wallace is his family. What we know almost for certain is that the Wallaces were not high nobles and did not possess any profound influence. What is accepted is that the Clan Wallace - or the Wallace family - was of landed gentry and had been established in Scotland for almost a century. However, in order to learn more about the Wallace family, we need to return back to the reign of Scottish King David I. He became King in 1124 AD, and before that point he spent much of his life abroad, in France and England. Due to this, he was quick to begin inviting Norman lords and noble families into Scotland, to follow on the already established practice of feudalism that was popular in England. As a monarch, he freely gave these Normans lands and ranks, increasing their military presence in Scotland and transforming regional lords into powerful noble families. In fact, many of the Scottish clans can trace their origins to these Norman knights that became powerful nobles in the service of David I. In fact, many of these landed knights would become the progenitors of the leading, ruling noble houses of Medieval Scotland. Some of these include the Bruces as the Lords of Annandale, the Balliols as rulers of Galloway, and the FitzAlans of Renfrew and Kyle, later to become the Stewarts. It is this latter family that is of interest to us in the story of William Wallace.

The FitzAlans came to Scotland from Shropshire, on the Welsh Marches, and with them they brought many of their vassals - small families of landed gentry that were in their service. Amongst these families was one that bore the surname Walays (or Wallace). This surname, clearly of interest to us, stems from the Old English word - *wylisc*, which denotes a "foreigner", or more commonly, a "Welshman". The surname appears in several versions, most commonly as Waleis, Walays, or Wallace. Arriving in Scotland, the Wallace family was given lands to hold in their service to the FitzAlans. Around this time is when we first find a historic document that bears the surname: one Walter FitzAlan found the great abbey of Paisley in 1163 AD. In the charter that confirmed this founding were signed several witnesses, amongst them one Richard Wallace, popularly taken to be an ancestor of William Wallace.

In time, the lesser family of Wallace held several estates in Scotland, most notably in the Kyle district of Ayrshire, between

Rivers Doon and Irvine. Furthermore, they held lands in Renfrewshire. This we learn from the later accounts of the bard Blind Harry (from whom a lot of Wallace's story stems), who also tells us that the father of William Wallace held lands at Auchenbothie and Elderslie. The latter place in Renfrewshire is most popularly associated with William Wallace and his father. However, there is no hard and substantial evidence that the Wallace family held the Elderslie estate prior to 1390, but there is also no evidence to suggest otherwise: it is quite possible that the estate was in their possession for generations prior to the emergence of William Wallace.

Another estate in their holding was Riccarton - itself a suburb of Kilmarnock in modern times - which lies in the district of Kyle in Ayrshire. Some scholars suggest that the place got its name from none other than the supposed ancestor of William Wallace, Richard Wallace. There is some sense in this suggestion, since Riccarton could have emerged from *Richards-tun, meaning Richard's Manor, later becoming Riccarton. Interestingly, there is a small memorial plaque in Riccarton today, at the entrance to the Fire Station. It states:

> *"Site of Riccarton Castle*
> *Birthplace of Malcolm Wallace*
> *Father of "Scotland's Hero"*

Riccarton Castle did exist in the village, although nothing of it remains today. Numerous stories and folktales regarding the castle and William Wallace are still retold in Riccarton to this day. However, scholars and historians know nothing for certain. Much that we just wrote about the origins of William Wallace is open to debate. For starters, it is uncertain what was the name of William Wallace's father. The most notable source that opens up the debate is the medieval chronicle of Scotichronicon, composed in the 1440s. In this chronicle is mentioned William Wallace - but in the space where his father's name should be is blank. From there, there are differing accounts. Some state that his father was named Andrew, while others name him Malcolm. The medieval poet, Blind Harry, in his tales of Wallace, states that his mother was Margaret Crawford of Corsbie, a small estate close to Troon in Ayrshire. Still, there exist no substantial evidence to confirm this. However, these maternal origins are widely accepted as true. In 1842, the Gazetteer of Scotland published a curious article related to Riccarton:

"Sir Ronald Crawford, the maternal uncle of Sir William Wallace, had, in this parish, a residence to which his illustrious nephew often resorted, and whence he sallied to perform many of the exploits which fame assigns him in the tales of tradition. The residence is said to have been a tower on the site of the farmhouse of Yardsides, immediately west of the village, but it has entirely disappeared, and has left, even in its vicinity, very doubtful memorials. A very ruinous and very humble edifice at the west end of a little row of cottages beside the farmhouse is pointed out as the barn which belonged to the tower, and, respectively in the garden and at the entrance to the farm yard are a pear tree which Wallace is said to have personally planted, and a very old tree perforated with an iron staple to which he fastened his horse when he visited the tower."

One limiting fact in the story of William Wallace is that of the narrative of Blind Harry. Plenty of what historians know today stems directly from the 15th century epic poem written by Blind Harry, called "The Wallace", or - *The Actes and Deidis of the Illustre and Vallyeant Campioun Schir William Wallace (Modern English: The Acts and Deeds of the Illustrious and Valiant Champion Sir William Wallace).* Written a century and a half after the life of William Wallace, the poem is full of historical inaccuracies, and mentions events that never happened. Nevertheless, it still contains some accurate information, albeit scarce. This fact had historians searching elsewhere, through the historical accounts, to piece together the life and deeds of William Wallace. Notably, the "Wallace" poem by Blind Harry became the most popular written work in Scotland, besides the Bible, and remained so for many generations. It was also used as the main inspiration for the popular Hollywood movie, "Braveheart", which retells a somewhat inaccurate tale of Wallace. The historian David R. Ross, perfectly sums it up:

"Blind Harry lived in the 1400s and wrote an epic poem extolling the virtues of Wallace. Much of it is based on reality, but much is fantasy. It has been ignored by most historians as there are no other documents to back it up, but it is an essential tool in letting us see how the ordinary Scot has viewed Wallace down the ages. The fact that many old histories, records and gazetteers make reference to the work of Harry shows just how popular this book has been with generations of Scots over the centuries."

Because of this, much of what can be read about William Wallace is simply not true, and exaggerated, coming dangerously close to legends and fantasy. However, there exist historical certainties that help us find the true information about our hero. What we do know is that William Wallace was the middle of three brothers - he had an elder brother Malcolm, and a younger one, John. Contemporary English chronicles mention them, which gives us some hard historical facts to go on. Just like William, the other two brothers would eventually meet their demise at the hands of the English.

The next serious question mark lies above the birthplace of William Wallace, which is still fiercely debated to this very day. In the past several years, several noted historians made claims that William Wallace was born in Ayrshire. There is a lot of confusion surrounding the birthplace and origins of William. Blind Harry tells us that William's father was "Malcolm Wallace, then of Ellerslie". It is this name that causes much confusion amongst scholars, as there exist two villages, Ellerslie and Elderslie - both claiming that they are the birthplace of Scotland's great hero. Furthermore, there are many claims of Ayrshire as the birthplace, specifically Craigie Castle. There exist ruins of that castle in the modern-day village of Craigie, situated between Ayr and Kilmarnock. Truly, the castle did belong to the Wallace family - but not before 1371. Chronicles tell us that in that year, a certain John Wallace married an heiress of the Lindsay family, and inherited Craigie Castle - its properties and titles - through that marriage. William Wallace was born around 1270 - nearly a century earlier - which makes that claim redundant. This brings us back to the historic mentions of Wallace as the Knight of either Ellerslie or Elderslie. Both names have the exact same meaning, denoting a "field of the elder trees". The village of Elderslie lies close to the city of Paisley in Renfrewshire, while a toponym of Ellerslie exists near Kilmarnock. Both have been cited as Wallace's birthplace. However, the latter does not appear on maps under the name of "Ellerslie" before 1835. Since the Wallace family, in their service to the Stewarts, ruled over Elderslie since at least 1250, and possessed a castle there (Auchenbothie Castle is quite near Elderslie), it is quite possible that this was, in fact, the actual birthplace of our hero. The confusion could arise from the original writings of Blind Harry, who wrote in the Old Scots dialect - where Elderslie was written as "Elrisle". Later transcriptions could have mistakenly translated it as Ellerslie.

The belief is that Elderslie was the family's possession from the mid-1200s, although official records show Wallaces as the owners from roughly 1390. From that point on, it remained in Wallace hands for 12 generations, across the centuries. In the twelfth generation, the only living child was a woman - one Helen Wallace, who ended up marrying Archibald Campbell, of Succoth and Garscube. Thus, the properties ended up in different hands, sold to a third person, one Alexander Speirs, a Glaswegian merchant. After several generations in that family, the Elderslie estate changed hands again, and the castle itself no longer exists. Contemporary medieval maps show Elderslie as a fenced stronghold, close to the Alt Patrick Water. In the late 1700s, excavations at this place revealed a stone bearing an inscription: "*W.W.W. Christ is only my redeemer*". It is believed that these initials refer to William Wallace and his father. There is further evidence of Wallaces in Elderslie. On the rising grounds above that Alt Patrick Water is a modern house that bears the name "Moat House". There is little doubt that this name is a corruption of the previous placename - Moot House, which signified a medieval fortified "motte and bailey tower". It is possible that this was the location of the Elderslie Castle that Wallaces held. In the gardens of this house are visible remains of defensive earthworks, as well as some stones that are undoubtedly ancient. Furthermore, there is a gnarled old yew tree nearby, undoubtedly very old, which bears the name "Wallace Yew". Local legends state that the tree is at least 700 years old, and that it once hid William Wallace in its canopy. Whether or not this is true, remains unknown. However, all these place names and toponyms suggest that Elderslie was - in fact - the birthplace of Scotland's celebrated hero.

Another similar tree stood in Elderslie and had much greater provenance. It was an exceptionally large and old oak tree, known locally as the "Wallace Oak", and reputedly planted in 1100. The connection with the tree and the Wallace surname goes back many generations, and it is possible that it dates to the Middle Ages. The legend states that the canopy was large enough to hide William Wallace and a contingent of his men from a marauding English patrol. The tree was so popular and connected with William Wallace, that souvenir hunters, in their thousands, cut small pieces of the tree to make souvenirs and snuff boxes. This eventually led to the tree looking barren and devastated, until it finally fell over in the late 1800s. In the end, all of these curiosities point to the fact that Elderslie was the birthplace of William Wallace, and also the place of his growing up. However, there are no definite proofs to confirm this, as no documents such as birth certificates existed at the time. Until a better theory appears, Elderslie is as good a guess as we can get.

Chapter II

Although William Wallace was born into a family of lesser nobility - that held little influence and moderate estates - he still had a better upbringing than some. It is likely that he received some education in his father's estates, most likely by a clergyman. This could have given him knowledge in Latin. Just like Robert the Bruce, Wallace would also have been multilingual, undoubtedly speaking Scots Gaelic, English, and the Scots dialect. However, we must take into account that William's "world" was much narrower and smaller than that of Robert the Bruce, his contemporary. We can safely assume that William Wallace never set foot outside of Scotland before his role in the war with England, and that most of his contacts were rather limited, centered on the region of his family's estates. Of course, these limitations likely stemmed from the quite strict hierarchical nature of the Scottish society of the time: Wallace had limited knowledge of great and powerful men of the time, and it is possible that powerful lords such as Bruce or Stewart carried more weight than that of the Scottish monarch, Alexander III. The latter came to the throne in 1249, well before William was born, and Scotland was in a fairly stable situation during his reign. In fact, in the generations following Alexander, the people of Scotland would look fondly on his reign, calling the period "the good old days". Most importantly, Scotland was largely unravaged by war - a welcome respite after many difficult periods in the past.

After the critical Battle of Largs, the Norwegians were effectively ousted out of Scotland, and the men and women of that nation could live in the peace that they yearned for. However, the death of a successful monarch almost always meant trouble in the realm. King

Alexander's first wife was Margaret of England - the sister of the then English King Edward Longshanks. From this marriage, the Scottish King was given two sons and a daughter. Alas, fate had it that they all died before their father - a tragic turn of events. With no heirs to the throne, Alexander realized that the fate of the realm was in question. Because of this, he married for the second time, after his first wife died in 1275 AD. His second wife was Yolande, the daughter of the powerful Comte de Dreux, whom he married in 1285. Alas, disaster only continued.

On March 18th, 1286, King Alexander III set out from Edinburgh Castle on a perilous night journey by horse. He rode with his small retinue, eager to reach Kinghorn Castle - in order to celebrate his wife's birthday, the next day. His advisors tried to urge him not to take the journey, but to no avail. The King rode hard and in treacherous terrain, in limited visibility, and with dangerous weather fast approaching. That would prove to be his ultimate mistake. During the perilous journey, the King got separated from his retinue in the darkness. They never saw him alive again: he was discovered on the following morning, at the bottom of a steep cliff, dead. His neck was broken, and he apparently fell from the cliff when his mount lost its footing in the dark. Thus, Scotland had lost - untimely - its King. That brought to the surface the question of succession. Thomas Napier Thompson, in his biography of this king, writes:

"...riding along a precipitous road between Bruntisland and Kinghorn, his horse fell over a rock, and the unfortunate monarch was killed. This event took place on the 16th of March 1286, in the 45th year of his age and 37th of his reign. With Alexander III terminated a race of kings, who, from the accession of Malcolm Cean-Mohr, had distinguished themselves by their activity in the administration of justice, and their

courage in maintaining the rights and independence of their country against a powerful and too often an insidious foe. Few annals of a rude people, indeed, can present a more remarkable series of patriotic monarchs than those with whom Scotland was blessed from the middle of the eleventh to the close of the thirteenth century, whether we consider their wisdom and impartiality as legislators, their prudence as politicians, or their bravery as warriors [...] But with the death of Alexander III, the peace and prosperity of the country was broken up; and much as he was lamented by the people, and gloomy as were their forebodings on his decease, no anticipation could exceed the real calamities in which the country was involved by his unhappy and untimely end."

It is likely that the hero of our story, William Wallace, was but a boy of twelve at this point. It is likely he was not even aware of the events that were unfolding in Scotland at the time. However, most would know that the King was dead. The more important matter lay in the question of succession. The King's distant relative, a young girl called Margaret the Maid of Norway, was the only potential heir to the throne. She too would not come to sit on it - she would die on Orkney sometime later, without ever arriving in Scotland proper.

As you can guess, the lack of an adequate heir to the throne of a kingdom leaves plenty of room for conflict. This conflict almost instantly erupted in Scotland after the young girl was dead. Without a legitimate successor, the throne was ripe for the taking. Due to this, potential claimants stepped forward, each one boasting a far-reaching connection to some of the previous kings of Scotland. There were thirteen of these claimants, each one saying that his claim was the strongest of all. To examine these claims, one has to go back to the reigns of Malcolm IV the Maiden, and his brother William the Lion. Neither of these kings left heirs, but their younger brother

- David Earl of Huntingdon - did. He had three daughters, and their relatives now sprang forth. One claimant was John Balliol - the grandson of one of these daughters (the eldest one), while another was Robert Bruce (grandfather of Robert the Bruce, King of Scots), who was the son of the second daughter. These two were the strongest and most legitimate claims to the throne. However, a great rivalry existed between Bruce and Balliol - a rivalry that threatened to plunge Scotland into a bitter civil war. It is around this time that the conflict between England and Scotland emerges - the conflict that is crucial to the story of William Wallace.

With civil war looming dangerously close, the Scots realized that they needed outside mediation in order to settle the question of the successor to the throne. Wanting to stop potential bloodshed, the Bishop of St. Andrews, William Fraser, wrote a letter to the English King Edward, asking for his intervention. The English King was in fact the brother-in-law of the late King Alexander, and his mediation in the matter seemed a natural course of action. However, Edward was quick to take advantage of the situation. He accepted the proposal and traveled north to Scotland in order to personally choose the rightful claimant to the throne. He met the leading Scotsmen at Norham Castle in May of 1291. There, he was quick to *demand* that they all accept his sovereignty and name him their overlord - i.e., the Lord Paramount of Scotland. Eventually, the gathered Scots acknowledged Edward as their overlord, and the latter proceeded to concern himself with the matter of succession at great length. After some considerate deliberation, Edward decided that it was, after all, John Balliol who was the rightful heir to the Scottish throne. It was the rightful decision, as Edward knew that Balliol had the strongest claim under the laws of the day, being the senior in genealogical primogeniture - descending from the eldest daughter of the Earl of Huntingdon, David. His decision was, perhaps, also influenced by the somewhat pliant nature of Balliol - he was perhaps not as strong a "player" as Robert the Bruce. John Balliol emerged from relative obscurity, and little is known of his early life.

As soon as he appointed Balliol to the throne, the English King began with his arrogant and somewhat humiliating demands. In every possible way, he demanded that the Scots be subjected to him - he acted from the start as the ruler of Scotland. He requested that Balliol personally travel to England and swear homage to him, and that the Scottish Lords send their own soldiers to fight English wars in France. All this created great pressures and unrest in Scotland. Balliol eventually stood his ground: in 1295 he resigned his homage to the English King, and instead turned to France, allying with this great enemy of England, and commencing a lasting alliance that would later be known as the "Auld Alliance". It was at this point that the Scottish Wars of Independence were about to erupt. Angered by the Scottish "betrayal" and their alliance with France, King Edward invaded Scotland. He was at the head of one of Europe's finest war machines - a seasoned army from the wars with France, with skilled commanders who forged their skills on the field of battle. The Scots, on the other hand, had something far more precious: a burning desire for freedom and independence from age-old English pressures.

Chapter III

It is time that we turn back to the early life of William Wallace - an early life of which history does not know all that much. We know that Wallace was a younger son. In medieval times, younger sons had little prospects in terms of succeeding their father's holdings, and often had to search for their fortunes elsewhere. Thus, we can safely say that William Wallace had an uncertain future at best. He was not prepared - by birth, provenance, or education - for any lofty roles in the unfolding destiny of his proud nation. Fate had it, that just within a year of the Wars of Scottish Independence, William Wallace was to play a decisive role that would cement his name onto the pages of the history books. Before we delve deeper into the life and deeds of William Wallace, we must once again reflect on his somewhat humble origins. As we said, the Wallace family likely originates from the region of the Welsh Marches and had traveled northwards with David I, in search of better prospects. The surname Wallace is most certainly coming from the Old English word "waelisc", that from the Anglo-Norman word "waleis", both meaning "a foreigner", or a "Welshman". It was a common word used as an umbrella term for Britons who came northwards into Scotland, most commonly in the 11th century, during the reign of David I. From that point on, the name of the Wallace family can be spotted relatively often in Ayrshire and Renfrewshire areas, where they are known to have held lands and estates.

The family most likely started with one Richard Wallace, whose name survived in the town and parish of Riccarton (Richard's Town). From Richard Wallace, we can reconstruct the family tree preceding William Wallace - although not with 100% certainty. The grandson of that Richard had two sons: Adam, the 4th Laird of Riccarton, and Malcolm, who received the lands of Auchinbothie in Elderslie, and Eldershire. This Malcolm received a knighthood and is commonly cited as the father of William Wallace. However, some confusion surrounds the matter. One surviving letter that William Wallace wrote himself, addressed to the mayor of Lübeck, Germany, and written on October 11th, 1297, bears the personal seal of Sir William Wallace. On it is displayed a symbol of a bow and arrow, and an inscription that states: WILLELMVS FILIVS ALANI WALAIS. This translates to "William, son of Alan Wallace". It is unclear to which Alan Wallace this refers, but the mention creates a mystery over the true parentage of William. There is one Alan Wallace that is mentioned in the 1296 Ragman Rolls, as a crown tenant from Ayrshire who is amongst the men who made their submission to King Edward. Because of this odd fact, historians of today are generally divided in their views of Wallace's parentage: for all we know it could be either Malcolm or Alan Wallace. If the first one was his father, then that would place his area of provenance to Elderslie. If it is the latter, though, then Wallace would hail from Ayrshire.

The version that is commonly found in most books and articles related to Wallace tells us that it is Malcolm Wallace who is his father. Either way, we can safely say that he was born between 1270 and 1276, and likely led a humble and peaceful life as a younger son of a lesser nobleman. However, we can also safely assume that his family's plans were altogether different than the life he was to lead later. A landless younger son with next to no prospects of success, William Wallace was likely destined for priesthood. Several facts point to this, and he might have spent some time in his early childhood preparing for a life of "the cloth". Alas, nature had different plans. It is said that William was an exceptionally large, muscular, and strong young boy and man. Such a promising future warrior was hardly destined for a clergyman's life. Still, history does not remember much of William's early childhood, and we can only guess at how it developed.

Many historians suggest that William had previous military experience before he stepped up into the pages of history at the onset of the Scottish Wars of Independence. As a younger son, he could have sought his fortunes abroad, fighting as a mercenary soldier, perhaps in Wales or England. Since his personal seal bore a symbol of a bow and arrow, we might suppose that he was employed as an archer in his youth, perhaps in the English King Edward's campaigns in Wales. Either way, we know that he was not a stranger to warfare once he appeared.

Some sources go on to state that his father, Sir Malcolm Wallace, and his eldest brother, both died at Irvine, likely in 1297, in one of the skirmishes against the English. This could have given William the necessary urge to continue his fight against the English even when many Scottish nobles submitted. Others give the year as 1291. William Wallace is first attested seriously in the pages of history following the Ragman Roll of 1296. It was this document, with which the English King Edward attempted to subjugate the whole of Scotland, which pushed William Wallace into a life of an outlaw. Whoever would refuse to sign his name in the rolls and do homage to Edward, was seen as an outlaw. When it came to the region of Ayrshire, Wallace's home, the responsibility for administering authority fell to Sir Ranald Crawford, who happened to be the maternal grandfather of William Wallace, and the Sheriff of Ayrshire. Now, it happened to be that the names of Sir Malcolm Wallace and his sons were not on the list of those who submitted, and that meant some severe penalties at the hands of the English. To save his kinsmen from English retribution, Crawford decided to take his daughter and her younger sons, William included, under his care and guardianship, but Malcolm Wallace and his eldest son had to flee to the north. Later on, Crawford sends his daughter and the boys to Kilspindie Castle in Perth and Kinross, where they were kept safe by one of the uncles of William Wallace, perhaps his mother's brother. An article from the Ordnance Gazetteer of Scotland (1882–84) written by Francis Groome, states of the village the following:

"Kilspindie, a village and a parish in Gowrie district, SE Perthshire. The village, standing in the mouth of a small glen, 1 mile SSW of Rait, 2⅛ miles NNW of Errol station, and 3⅜ NNE of Glencarse station, had anciently a castle, now extinct, and figures in Blind Harry's narrative as the place where Sir William Wallace, with his mother, found refuge in his boyhood."

Here, it is said that Wallace continued his education, likely in Dundee, now being roughly 17 or 18 years of age. Some early friendships were formed then, which would last for years and continue even during William's exploits in the war. He met one John Blair, a young Benedictine monk who would be alongside William as a comrade in arms, as well as Sir Neil Campbell of Lochawe and Duncan of Lorn. The names of these men would be mentioned in connection with Wallace's early exploits.

These accounts, of course, are not necessarily the true historical fact: as we said, much is speculated about William Wallace, and he could have been employed as a mercenary for some time before becoming known in Scotland's affairs. Nevertheless, we know that around this time William's first troubles with the English begin. There are many semi-legendary accounts related to this. One such legend states that young William Wallace was bullied and challenged by the son of the English governor of the Castle in Dundee - one Selby. William then killed him "with a single blow" and then went into hiding. There is no evidence of this. Also uncertain is William's purported marriage to one Marion Braidfute, the 18-year-old daughter of Sir Hugh Braidfute of Lamington. The legends state that William fell in love with her, and that the two planned to get married. However, the English murdered Marion in 1297, which prompted William's retribution and rebellion against the English forces. There is, however, no historical documentation to confirm any of this, and it could have all been a romantic invention in later retellings of Wallace's deeds.

Chapter IV

There is no doubt that William Wallace was destined for great deeds, and that he was the epitome of a true Highlander Scottish warrior. Life of priesthood was not destined for him, and we can safely assume that he was a skilled warrior employed as a mercenary. When the time came to exchange blows with the English invaders, William Wallace was in his prime - and eager to fight. Numerous accounts - some near-contemporary and some later - tell us that William was a large and powerful man. While the poet Blind Harry says that he was seven feet tall, another account by Walter Bower states:

"He was a tall man with the body of a giant, cheerful in appearance with agreeable features, broad-shouldered and big-boned, with belly in proportion and lengthy flanks, pleasing in appearance but with a wild look, broad in the hips, with strong arms and legs, a most spirited fighting-man, with all his limbs very strong and firm."

The legends of his great stature endured in folk tales, and it is quite possible that he indeed was larger than what was usual at the time. A two-handed great sword survives today, and is named the "Wallace Sword", alleged to have belonged to the hero. The gigantic sword measures over five feet including the hilt and it is rather heavy. If it is an indication of Wallace's stature, then the man must have been truly powerful and large. However, modern research cannot confirm the true provenance of the sword, and it is disputed that it ever did belong to the hero. Either way, we can safely say that William Wallace was the true example of a robust Scottish warrior, whose great stature would instill fear into the hearts of the English.

In May of 1297 AD, William Wallace first entered onto the stage of history - in earnest. This is the first act that we definitely know was carried out by Wallace, and one of the series of uprisings and small actions aimed against the English. This was the true start of the Scottish War of Independence, and Wallace was one of the several Scottish nobles who decided to stand their ground and take up arms.

In May of 1297, William Wallace murdered William de Heselrig, the English High Sheriff of Lanark. This event is known today as the Action at Lanark. Not much is known about this event, and it is still not known whether it was an isolated incident, or an event coordinated with other such sporadic revolts across Scotland.

Not much is known with certainty about Wallace's famed action at Lanark. Much of what was "reconstructed" in the popular movie "Braveheart" is simply filled with the movie-maker's artistic freedom and can't be likened to real historic events. Either way, the attack on the English at Lanark was an event that resounded through the region, and quickly placed William Wallace's name at the forefront of Scottish happenings. Some tales speak of dramatic events that preceded this attack. One legend claims that Sheriff Heselrig wanted to invoke the practice of the "Prima Nocte," or the "First Night," meaning that he wanted to sleep with Wallace's wife on their wedding day. Others claim that Heselrig captured or even murdered Wallace's wife Marion, in order to provoke and lure out Wallace. Neither of these legendary claims can be confirmed with certainty. What we do know comes from the medieval chronicle of "Scalacronica," written by Thomas Grey. Grey's father, also named Thomas, was present at Lanark during these events, and survived Wallace's onslaught. According to "Scalacronica," a scuffle or a quarrel broke out at the Lanark court that was held by Heselrig. The nature of the quarrel is unknown, but we can safely assume that it did involve William Wallace - either directly or indirectly. The chronicle tells us that Wallace was able to flee from the ensuing chaos with the help of a woman, who might have been his wife. Subsequently, Wallace returned to Lanark - likely at the head of some 40 men - and gained his revenge. He attacked Lanark, killing Heselrig and many of his English troops, and setting several homes ablaze. All these centuries after, we are not sure what Wallace was doing at Lanark or how this clash arose. Some propose that it was a deliberate attack coordinated with other such risings in Scotland, while others stick to the theory that it was simply an isolated and spontaneous incident. Either way, it was this event that started Wallace's legendary rebellion, and paved the way toward his other major achievements. Lanark was a spark that started Wallace's flame: at first it was faint, but soon enough it was a roaring blaze that every patriotic Scotsman could feel and see.

Following this attack, William Wallace and his band of men fled into hiding, most likely to the north of Lanark, into the Torwood forest. From here, they led a guerilla campaign against the English. According to the epic poem of Blind Harry, it was because of these guerilla tactics of Wallace that the English King decided to hang several of the Scottish barons of Ayrshire - in an event called the Barns of Ayr. Today, the authenticity of this event is disputed, although there are some sporadic mentions of it. If it did occur, it could have happened in 1306, after William Wallace was dead. Nevertheless, popular tales state that William Wallace attacked the English garrison in Ayr - in order to avenge the executed barons. He trapped the English soldiers in a barn and set it ablaze: any soldiers who fled were quickly cut down.

Either way, the dice was cast. After Lanark, William Wallace was an outlaw and a patriotic fighter against the English. He knew that there was no way out, no possible outcome other than victory or death. The English were sure to condemn him to death if they would capture him, so the only option he had left was to *fight*. In time, others like him joined his ranks. Scotsmen - both noble and commoner - came to the aid of William Wallace, lending him their swords and bodies.

One of the first to join up with Wallace was William the Hardy, Lord of Douglas, the father of the famed James "the Black" Douglas. More powerful nobles at first saw William Wallace as a lowborn outlaw and considered it beneath their dignity to join his ranks. The Lord of Douglas had no such issues and was eager to take up the fight. Initially, William the Hardy was summoned by the English King on July 7th, 1297, likely to swear homage and lend his sword to the Englishman's war. Douglas refused outright and took to the woods with Wallace. With their forces combined, Douglas and Wallace could now continue their revolt and strike at new English targets. Together they raided a number of English garrisons: at Sanquhar, Durisdeer, and Scone. The latter was the most significant attack of the three and is known as the Raid on Scone. It occurred in June 1297 and saw a major raid on that city. Wallace managed to take the English defenders by surprise, and the Justice of Scotland, the English-appointed William de Ormesby, barely escaped with his life, fleeing in panic. At Scone Abbey, Wallace gained possession of the English treasury, and thus made good use of the treasure he found there. After Scone, he had the necessary funds to continue his war effort. From there, he based his forces at Ettrick Forest, from where he continued to attack new English sites. He raided the manor of Robert Wishart, the Bishop of Glasgow, which was located at Ancrum, and later he attacked Dundee, possibly besieging it. Here, it is possible that he met and joined forces with Andrew Moray, who also led a revolt independent of Wallace. With their forces joined, the freedom fighters' ranks continued to swell.

Chapter V

By this point, William Wallace was one of Scotland's leading freedom fighters. Men far and wide heard of his exploits, and patriotic souls flocked to his side. However, his rise to prominence also attracted increased attention from the English. One of the lead men of Wallace's rank, the nobleman Sir John de Graham of Dundaff, obtained critical information that forced Wallace to shift his troops from the Selkirk Forest area towards the Highlands, north of Stirling. Throughout Scottish history, Stirling and its imposing castle both remained a critical junction and one of the most formidable spots in the realm. A highly important strategic position, it is popularly said that Stirling is the "Gateway to the Highlands", and "a huge brooch clasps the Highlands and Lowlands together". Furthermore, it is said that *he who owns Stirling, owns the whole of Scotland*. Due to all this, Wallace decided to march on Stirling. What ensued was one of the first major battles of the First Scottish War of Independence.

One year prior, the Scots suffered a great defeat at the Battle of Dunbar, at the hands of England's leading military commander and a prominent nobleman, John de Warenne, 6th Earl of Surrey. Now, Warenne joined up his forces with those of the overconfident and arrogant Hugh de Cressingham, his chief adviser and the man that was widely hated by both the Scots and the English. The two men arrived close to Stirling around September 9th, 1297. Warenne was now concerned with the number of men that the Scots fielded, and the positions of the two armies, which were separated by the River Forth that ran near Stirling Castle. The bridge was fordable over a long causeway and a quite narrow wooden bridge. It was said that three men could barely cross it abreast. Warenne knew that it would be a tactical disadvantage to take his army across, so he decided to stall before making the right decision. To that end, he sent envoys to negotiate with William Wallace. He sent James Stewart and two Dominican Friars to parlay with Wallace at Cambuskenneth Abbey, where they told the Scotsman to submit. Confident of his goals and his patriotism, William Wallace allegedly told them:

"Return to thy friends and tell them that we come here with no peaceful intent, but ready for battle, determined to avenge our wrongs and to set our country free. Let thy masters come and attack us; we are ready to meet them beard to beard!"

These words come from the poet Blind Harry, and they might have been blown out of proportion. However, it is not unlikely that Wallace said something of the sort, as another rendition from the 14th century chronicler Walter of Guisborough survives:

"We are not here to make peace but to do battle, to defend ourselves and liberate our kingdom. Let them come on and we shall prove this to their very beards."

All the while, the Scottish troops were positioned on top of a nearby hill, called the Abbey Craig, which allowed them to dominate the soft flat grounds to the north of the river. The English were, in contrast, positioned on the flat grounds to the south of the river. The English army numbered some 9,000 men, made up of 7,000 skilled infantry and 2,000 heavy cavalry. Amongst these troops were some prominent English noblemen, such as the above-mentioned Hugh de Cressingham, Sir Richard Waldegrave, and Sir Marmaduke Thweng, 1st Baron Thweng. In stark contrast, the Scottish army numbered between 5,300 and 6,300 men at the most, with roughly 5,000 to 6,000 infantry and just 300 cavalry.

As it seemed that a battle with William Wallace was inevitable, the English under the Earl of Surrey began looking for the best place to cross the river with their army, as to be able to confront the Scots. One of the men, a Scottish knight who joined the English ranks - Sir Richard Lundie - proposed to conduct a flanking maneuver. He said he knew a favorable crossing spot on the river, where sixty horsemen could cross at once. However, it was Hugh de Cressingham, the impulsive and arrogant English nobleman, who quickly rejected this advice and convinced the Earl of Surrey to use the wooden bridge instead. This crossing allowed for a direct attack and was also the safest crossing point. It was also the slowest and most tactically disadvantageous crossing, as the bridge was quite narrow and opened up on the marshy haws of Flanders Moss to the north of the river. It would later prove that Hugh de Cressingham's arrogance and hastiness would be quite costly to the English, as their choice was just the thing that William Wallace wanted. Patiently the Scotsmen waited, letting the English troops cross over. At their head were Cressingham, Marmaduke Thweng, and Sir Waldegrave - ignorant of what was about to ensue.

Wallace and his army carefully observed the English progress: it is said that they waited as much as they could, letting only enough English troops to cross as they could deal with. What followed next was the Battle of Stirling Bridge, fought on September 11th, 1297. Some solid details of the engagement come from the medieval Chronicle of Hemingburgh, written by Walter of Guisborough, who says that the English were slow to cross, hampered by the narrowness of the bridge. However, when a substantial number of English troops crossed, Wallace ordered the attack, confident in his superiority and the advantage of his troops. At the forefront of the attack were Wallace's skilled Scottish spearmen, who raced down the slope from their hillside positions, and swarmed over the English soldiers. They quickly dealt with a rushed counterattack of the English heavy cavalry, and then turned their attention towards the enemy infantry. What followed next was a true decimation of the English army. As the Scots gained possession of the eastern side of the bridge, they effectively eliminated any chance of English reinforcements crossing over. Those English troops that were caught in Wallace's trap on the low ground in the loop of the river were now helpless and lost. They were surrounded by the Scots and promptly butchered. Historians agree that most of these troops were killed, some in battle, some while fleeing in panic. Many also drowned trying to swim across the river, with only a few hundred reaching safety on the other shore. Sir Marmaduke Thweng was the only English knight to manage to flee back across the bridge. In fact, his heroic conduct gained him substantial fame following the battle: with a handful of soldiers, he fought his way across, and thus saved his own life. Seeing the carnage from the other side of the river, the Earl of Surrey was truly distraught. His confidence was shattered to pieces, seeing so many of his men butchered before his very own eyes. In fact, Surrey still commanded a strong position on the southern side of the river, having his contingent intact and strengthened with archers. However, his zeal was gone. Once the Earl of Surrey saw that Sir Marmaduke Thweng had escaped back across the bridge, he ordered the bridge to be destroyed, in order to deny the Scots an easy passage across. He then retreated towards Berwick, and thus left the small garrison at Stirling Castle isolated. With that, Surrey effectively abandoned the Scottish Lowlands, leaving them to the mercy of Wallace's patriots.

Also present at the Battle of Stirling Bridge were Scotsmen that were at the time loyal to the English King. These were James Stewart, the High Steward of Scotland, and Malcolm the Earl of Lennox. We can only imagine how mixed their feelings were as they watched their fellow Scotsmen butchering the clueless English troops which they had pledged loyalty to. Since they were, alas, on the opposing side, they also withdrew from the battlefield along with Surrey and Thweng. However, it seems as if they had a change of heart and realized where their true loyalties lay. As soon as they withdrew, they betrayed the Earl of Surrey and defected to Wallace's side. They attacked the English supply train at the place called The Pows, and inflicted further casualties on the fleeing English soldiers. With that, the Battle of Stirling Bridge was a complete and undeniable triumph for William Wallace and his Scotsmen. It was a surprising, lighting-strike victory that few expected so early in the Scottish War of Independence. With cunning and patience, Wallace struck at the overconfident English, crushing them to pieces in what was a complete butchery of the superior enemy army. Some contemporary accounts give a confident and detailed number of English troops that died on that day. Walter of Guisborough writes that 100 cavalry and 5,000 English infantry were killed. It was a catastrophic English loss and a major setback so early in the conflict. On the other hand, Scottish casualties likely numbered just a few hundred. However, one major leader of the rebellion was amongst the casualties: Andrew Moray, Wallace's chief ally, friend, and advisor, received a major wound during the fighting. He died some months later, towards the end of 1297. His death was a major loss for the Scottish cause, and especially for William Wallace, who is said to have greatly mourned the loss of his close ally.

However, the English lost some prominent figures at Stirling as well. The most notable casualty on their side was Sir Hugh de Cressingham, hated by many and loved by few. Several contemporary accounts write of his death. The chronicle of Pierre de Langtoft writes that Cressingham was *"unaccustomed to the saddle, and from his steed in its course fell under foot, His body was cut to pieces by the ribalds of Scotland"*. Furthermore, several accounts state that the Scots flayed him after the battle, just as he had the reputation of flaying and tormenting Scottish prisoners of war. The Lanercost Chronicle claims that Wallace had *"a broad strip [of Cressingham's skin] ... taken from the head to the heel, to make therewith a baldrick for his sword."* Others confirm this: *"The Scots flayed him and divided his skin among themselves in moderate-sized pieces, certainly not as relics, but for hatred of him".* It should not be surprising that Wallace indeed wore the piece of Cressingham's skin on his person, as the greatest trophy taken from his bitter enemies.

Following their victory at Stirling Bridge, William Wallace and his men continued to raid in the wake of the retreating English. They penetrated as far south as Durham in England and gained substantial loot by doing so. More importantly, William Wallace's reputation as the leading freedom fighter of Scotland was cemented. Together with Andrew Moray, he was named the Guardian of Scotland - and remained the sole Guardian once Moray died soon after. To make things official, William Wallace received his knighthood towards the end of 1297. This ceremony was conducted in Selkirk (The Kirk o' the Forest), by one of the three leading Scottish earls - Robert the Bruce (Earl of Carrick), Malise III the Earl of Strathearn, or Maol Choluim I, the Earl of Lennox. With that, *Sir* William Wallace became the *"Guardian of the kingdom of Scotland and commander of its army."*

Today, the River Forth near Stirling can be crossed via a 15th century stone bridge, built long after the heroic battle. However, the Stirling Bridge of Wallace's battle likely stood some 180 yards upstream from that location, today non-existent. Archeology, however, revealed four stone piers underwater, as well as man-made stonework on one bank. This was undoubtedly the site of the fierce fighting, and the area can still be observed today. Furthermore, on top of the Abbey Craig - the dominating hill where Wallace and his men hid - an epic monument has been erected. It is the iconic National Wallace Monument, dedicated to Scotland's great hero and the Battle of Stirling Bridge. A monumental 67-meter (220 feet) tower, it was completed in 1869, following a major fundraising campaign during a resurgence of Scottish national identity. The epic tower stands as a fundamental memory to Wallace's great achievement.

The triumph of William Wallace and his freedom fighters continued to live in the hearts of all Scots for generations after. Such a heroic undertaking brought a new spark of hope to the oppressed Scottish folk, and tales of Wallace's deeds were preserved by word of mouth from one generation to another. One of the most popular (and arguably the first) major written works that tells us of the Battle of Stirling Bridge is the epic poem of Blind Harry, "The Wallace". Written some 200 years after the battle, the poem was used to entertain the courtiers of James IV, and largely blends fact and fiction. However, the work brought great inspiration to all Scottish people. Still, we need to consider that the poet's account of the battle is highly improbable, and contains a lot of fictitious details, and parts that are blown out of proportion. Yet even so, Blind Harry's poem and his use of artistic freedom inspired generations of Scots - both young and old.

"On Saturday they [Moray and Wallace] rode on to the bridge, which was of good plain board, well made and jointed, having placed watches to see that none passed from the army. Taking a wright, the most able

workman there, he [Wallace] ordered him to saw the plank in two at the mid streit [middle stretch], so that no-one might walk over it. He then nailed it up quickly with hinges, and dirtied it with clay, to cause it to appear that nothing had been done. The other end he so arranged that it should lie on three wooden rollers, which were so placed, that when one was out the rest would fall down. The wright, himself, he ordered to sit there underneath, in a cradle, bound on a beam, to loose the pin when Wallace let him know by blowing a horn when the time was come. No one in all the army should be allowed to blow but he himself.

Hugh Cressingham leads on the vanguard with twenty thousand likely men to see. Thirty thousand the Earl of Warren had, but he did then as wisdom did direct, all the first army being sent over before him. Some Scottish men, who well knew this manner of attack, bade Wallace sound, saying there were now enough. He hastened not, however, but steadily observed the advance until he saw Warren's force thickly crowd the bridge. Then from Jop he took the horn and blew loudly, and warned John the Wright, who thereupon struck out the roller with skill; when the pin was out, the rest of it fell down. Now arose an hideous outcry among the people, both horses and men, falling into the water. (...)

On foot and bearing a great sharp spear, Wallace went amongst the thickest of the press and aimed a stroke at Cressingham in his corslet, which was brightly polished. The sharp head of the spear pierced right through the plates and through his body, stabbing him beyond rescue; thus, was that chieftain struck down to death. With the stroke Wallace bore down both man and horse.

The English army although ready for battle, lost heart when their chieftain was slain and many openly began to flee. Yet, worthy men abode in the place until ten thousand were slain. Then the remainder fled, not able to abide longer, seeking succour in many directions, some east, some west and some fled to the north. Seven thousand full at once floated in the Forth, plunged into the deep and drowned without mercy; none were left alive of all that fell army."

Chapter VI

For William Wallace, things have turned to better almost overnight. His monumental victory brought Scotland back up to its feet, and the majority of leading Scottish nobles immediately swung to support him. Stirling Bridge was the sign they needed - a sign to once and for all throw away the oppressive shackles of the English. The victory gave Wallace the Guardianship over Scotland, and the new initiative to counterattack on the English, leading raids into their own territory, late in 1297. In fact, the whole of the north of England was opened up for him, as the badly beaten Earl of Surrey retreated hastily and deeply - all the way to York. This was done contrary to the plans of the English King Edward. By September 21st, 1297, the Exchequer in London received reports of the death of Hugh de Cressingham. By September 24th, King Edward sent instructions from Flanders, trying to quickly remedy the situation. He ordered the Earl of Surrey to remain in Scotland and to be reinforced by the army of Robert Clifford, the Sheriff of York, and thirteen nobles of England's north. However, the news traveled slowly, and executing these orders was by that point impossible - by September 27th, the Earl of Surrey had retreated to York leaving the north free to the Scottish raids.

Not at all surprisingly, the folk of the northern English regions were struck with blind panic. Knowing that Wallace and his fierce highland warriors were descending upon them - drunk on their victory at Stirling - these folk quickly abandoned their homes. Walter of Guisborough, in his chronicle, sums it up:

"For the Northumbrians were petrified with fear, and they evacuated from the countryside their wives and children and all their household

goods, sending them with their animals to Newcastle and various other places throughout the provinces."

However, Wallace was not quick to act, as rashness could have been costly at this time. Because of this, the invasion of northern England did not begin at once. Historical accounts of this period are scant and lacking, but we can still piece together the puzzle and try to reconstruct his movements.

The first reports of Scottish activity in the North of England were first documented in October of 1297, on the 13th. What William Wallace did in the weeks between Stirling and this date, we can only reconstruct based on later chronicles. We know that after Stirling, he chose to pursue the retreating Earl of Surrey, perhaps in order to capitalize on his victory. He chased the English Earl and his troops all the way to Hutton Moor, a place outside of Berwick. Here he halted and stopped his chase - and he observed the new English positions arrayed ready to fight him. Wallace did not approach Berwick because of this, and retreated to the Duns Park area, where he rested his troops. There are also suggestions that he then turned northwards in an attempt to continue the siege of Dundee Castle. He certainly had time for this. Still, as we already said, the Earl of Surrey did not linger - he was quick to flee from Scotland. Berwick was thus ripe for the taking, and we can safely say that it was occupied by the Scots some time before October 11th. It was on this date that William Wallace wrote a letter to the mayors and commons of the Hanseatic cities of Hamburg and Lubeck, informing them that the Scottish port was once more open for their ships and for new business. Still, it is likely that the castle of Berwick was not assaulted and remained garrisoned by the English even though the town was de facto Scottish. We know that William Wallace sent Henry de Haliburton to take possession of the town, only once the

English residents abandoned it. With Berwick occupied, Wallace could now face the north of England. The medieval Lanercost chronicle sums it up thus:

"After this [the capture of Berwick] the Scots gathered together and invaded, devastating the whole country, causing burnings, depredations and murders, and they came almost up to the town of Newcastle, but turned away from it and invaded the county of Carlisle; there they did as in Northumberland, destroying everything, and afterwards they returned to Northumberland, to devastate more fully anything they had overlooked previously; and on the feast of St. Cecilia virgin and martyr they returned to Scotland."

The great hero of Scotland, William Wallace, was now in the position to be the one to wreak havoc and revenge - that same revenge that the Scots yearned for, for so long. That revenge was to be exacted upon the undeserving folk of northern England. Near contemporary accounts tell us that Wallace began raiding around October 18th, on the day of the feast of St. Luke, when Northumberland felt the Scots' wrath. However, it is certain that a massed, concentrated, and planned invasion by Wallace did not begin in earnest until at least November 11th, around the day of the feast of St. Martin. Scattered bands of raiders and marauders likely invaded in October, with Wallace following with his army in November. Either way, their wrath was unchecked. The Scots seem to have been based in Rothbury Forest, roughly halfway between Berwick and Newcastle, from where they could conduct their raids and operations. The earliest Scottish action in Northumberland that is positively dated is the burning of the Felton Mill, close to Rothbury, which occurred around October 13th, a fortnight after Michaelmas. All across the region, the folk fled from their countryside homes, seeking refuge in castles and walled towns, as

Wallace and his men raided. The English response, in the meantime, was rather slow. London was aware of the Scottish incursions, chiefly because by that point the Earl of Surrey had arrived to inform them of the events. The only resistance that Wallace and his men encountered came from the local castles and their garrisons. Most notable was the garrison of Alnwick castle, who kept harassing the raiders where they could. However, nothing major could be done: the King was absent from the court, being in Flanders at that time. By October 23rd, Westminster was issuing orders for a general muster against the Scottish invaders, but the mobilization on a mass scale took time, and the muster would not occur until early December.

The Scots, of course, did not hesitate to burn, pillage, and loot the poorly defended northern areas. A sharp decrease in rents and tithes in certain villages tells us that the Scottish attacks mostly came from the direction of Berwick. Many villages, mills, and manors were laid to waste and burned, causing great damage to the lords and barons who owned them. Around mid-November, the main Scottish army is recorded arriving, which is connected with William Wallace and his men. Further villages were abandoned or laid to waste, and Newcastle was prepared for an imminent attack. Its castle had a garrison of 88 crossbowmen, 88 archers, and 6 men-at-arms, all ready for the worst. However, it seems that Wallace was not interested in Newcastle, perhaps considering an attack too costly for his men. There was thus no attack on Newcastle, and Wallace seemingly bypassed it intentionally. Instead, he moved his forces towards Tynedale. There they devastated Bywell, and the surviving documents tell us that nearly half of the demesne - 103 acres out of 235 - was laid to waste and remained so for the rest of the year. Corbridge was also burned and devastated, and by November,

Wallace was at Hexham Priory which apparently escaped destruction by paying the Scots a ransom. Two letters written by William Wallace document this. Still, his forces continued moving.

The next target of Wallace's raids was Carlisle. Accounts were kept at the time by the Bishop of Carlisle, the keeper of Carlisle Castle, who writes that on Martinmas, both the city and the castle were besieged by the great Scottish army. It is also stated that William Wallace, upon arriving in Carlisle, sent a clerk to its citizens demanding that they surrender in the name of "William the Conqueror". The town leaders refused, and subsequently William Wallace did not attempt to storm it. Such an endeavor would, surely, have been costly to his men, as the town was equipped with machines to resist a siege. When the Scots marched away, they devastated many sites on their path, laying waste to places such as the forest of Inglewood, Cumberland, Allerdale, and Derwent at Cockermouth.

Oddly enough, no considerable resistance was given to the Scots while they conducted their raids. This is certainly confusing once you take into account the fact that the county possessed of both Cumberland and Lancashire should have been active and ready to oppose William Wallace, since they were disbanded even before the Battle of Stirling. Still, there exists substantial evidence that the English did make attempts to raise an army which would oppose the raiders. Contemporary accounts record an incident that occurred on November 10th at Sowerby, where an arrayer was sent by the noble Robert Clifford to assemble all footmen at Carlisle that were capable of bearing arms . When one man refused to join up, he was flat out murdered. This might be evident that the English were desperate to raise an effective fighting force to oppose Wallace on their land.

By mid-November, William Wallace's army was reformed and joined up by a force of Galwegians - and it then marched back into the Tynedale area. According to the medieval chronicles of Walter of Guisborough, the Scots contemplated invading Durham, but "St. Cuthbert, in the week after Martinmas, sent snowstorms in which many of the Scots perished". At this point, we should not doubt the fact that winter weather did hamper the Scottish raiders, and many could have died from exposure. Another fact that might have prevented Wallace from marching on Durham is the spread of false rumors that the Bishop of Durham assembled a great host to defend his city. Walter of Guisborough himself points out that such rumors were false, as Durham contributed immensely in terms of animals, resources, and men for the preceding English actions in Scotland. Thus, Durham was defenseless at the time, unbeknownst to William Wallace. Instead, Wallace chose to return to Hexham Priory, which he visited months before. Close to Newcastle, the priory served as a good base of operations for the Scottish army and offered protection from the increasingly challenging winter weather.

Around this time, a certain anecdote occurs, which was recorded by the pen of Walter of Guisborough. He writes that only three canons were left at the Hexham Priory, with others all evacuated before the Scots arrived. Walter writes that the men of the Scottish army continually harassed these clergymen, demanding to be shown the priory's hidden treasures. One of the clergymen replied, *"It is not a long time since your people carried off almost everything of ours to your own country, so where it is kept you know very well."* This was likely a nudge to the Scottish raids of the previous year, which happened in June 1296, when the Scots plundered the priory. Here, an interesting relationship between William Wallace and his men is shown. At one point, Wallace arrived at the priory and demanded from the clergymen to hear Mass. While he left the church to discard his weapons, since Mass could not be attended with them, his men plundered the altar and stole the precious sacred vessels. Wallace was greatly angered by this event and also embarrassed. Because the theft was sacrilegious, Wallace at once demanded to know who the perpetrators of the crime were and threatened to punish all men severely. He reportedly apologized to the clergymen, saying that *"these were a rough and uncivilized people, who had no shame."* Historians agree that it was likely the Galwegians who stirred up trouble and committed the crime. However, we are left with the question of Wallace's authority, and his personal relationship with the men of his army. Was Wallace's partially noble provenance the fact that set him apart from the common Highlander of the time? Most important of all: was Wallace's army a regular, disciplined army of Scotland, or a band of roving raiders with little to no discipline? These are some of the questions that remain to be answered.

For two days, William Wallace used the Hexham Priory as his base of operations, raiding the surrounding countryside in the meantime. However, even though the onset of winter was now fast approaching, and the weather was freezing, the Scottish army abandoned the shelter that the priory provided and continued their march along the Tyne river, towards Newcastle. Reports of several villages on the river being destroyed are dated to this time. One interesting anecdote is preserved related to this, and it involves the men from the village of Ryton, near Durham. As the river Tyne was at the time swelling with water and wild, they thought that the Scots - who were on the opposite side - could not reach them. Due to this, they mocked, jeered, and teased the Scottish soldiers. However, they were struck with blind panic when a group of daring Scots decided to swim across the turbulent waters and raze their village to the ground.

Either way, Wallace was intent on marching towards Newcastle, perhaps to see whether he could assail it or not. The city, however, expecting an attack, refurbished its defenses and maintained a modest garrison. It is likely that William Wallace was impressed by the town's defenses and thought that an attack or a prolonged siege would not end well for his troops. Of course, we need to consider the possible fact that the winter weather, the cold and the hunger, all affected his men. Then there is the fact that the Scots simply did not want to risk losing all their spoils in a big battle. Very soon after, perhaps in late November, Wallace and the main bulk of his army returned across the border and into Scotland, having achieved no major objective. In the end, Wallace did not commit to attacking any major city. In fact, his entire campaign in England in the winter of 1297 boiled down to nothing but raiding and pillaging, roughly in the area between Carlisle and Newcastle. It is documented, however, that before they left England, they attacked and pillaged Mitford Castle.

Alas, before the close of 1297, the Scots already lost all of the initiative they had built after the victory at Stirling Bridge. Just before the year was out, around Christmas, Robert Clifford led a raid into Annandale. Then a couple of months later, by February of 1298, the Earl of Surrey- bolstered by the Lords of Northumberland and Cumberland - raised the Scottish siege of Roxburgh and once more recaptured Berwick.

In the end, there is a lot to learn about William Wallace and his *modus operandi* from this semi-fruitful raid of England's north. The historical significance of the raid is - certainly - questionable, as are some of his actions and uncertainties. The most important fact to consider here is that William's raids had - arguably - no lasting long term economic effects on northern England. Of course, some of the affected bishoprics and townships had a struggle to survive and recuperate in the years immediately after Wallace's raids. After all, contemporary accounts paint a stark picture of ruthless medieval warfare: people were driven from their homes, entire communities were displaced, major economic buildings such as barns, mills, and townhouses, were burned to the ground, growing crops were trampled, herds, flocks and oxen were driven off en-masse. All of this was significant in the middle ages. Still, the area was given a period of respite after this episode, and certainly had time to recover. Once William Wallace was out of England, the region had almost a decade of respite: new raids occurred sporadically only in 1307, and in earnest in 1315.

With all of that being said, it becomes increasingly difficult for historians to deduce the exact nature of Wallace's operation. The course of his actions gives little logic: the entire campaign was reduced down to a wandering course from east to west, between Newcastle and Carlisle. Even more puzzling is the fact that he did nothing when arriving to either town, showing major indecisiveness. The surviving documents and chronicles clearly tell us that Wallace had a great interest in these strategic cities: but once before them, he made no attempts at siege or assault. Furthermore, his failure to take on other poorly defended English cities or to confront any lesser English army in the open field has long been debated amongst historians. Some scholars have proposed a challenge to Wallace's authority and suggested that the difficulties in the campaign came from the ranks. Perhaps it was the lack of discipline that hindered Wallace's success in the raids. Such a lack of discipline is hinted at by the medieval chronicles, such as the anecdote from the Hexham Priory. Another evidence is the surviving anecdote of the events before Newcastle. Upon arriving there, Wallace's army did not conduct any operations, but instead shared out all the loot, before departing - with the Glaswegians going their own way, and the rest of the army to the north. All this led historians to assume that the lack of discipline greatly hampered William Wallace and prevented him from capitalizing on his victory at Stirling Bridge.

Chapter VII

By the Spring of 1298, the English war machine was revving up its engine for a new, renewed attack on Scotland. By all accounts, their devastating defeat at Stirling Bridge came as a surprise but did not halt them for good - as could be expected. So, in April of that year, King Edward ordered a second invasion of Scotland. This time, he'd make sure that no mistakes happened. Because of this, he assembled a vast army of some 25,000-foot soldiers, and 1,500 cavalry, plus archers. It was a massive army, which entered Scotland at Roxburgh and proceeded to plunder and devastate Lothian, regaining some of the lost castles there. However, the English failed to lure William Wallace out to battle. The Scots kept out running them, adopting a scorched earth policy in order to deprive the English of resources and to keep their morale low. Wallace's goals here were rather cunning, and well thought out. He intended to avoid the English army, dragging their pursuit out until they'd run out of supplies. When the English would be forced to retreat back, he'd swing around and harass their retreat. Things did not go according to plan. By July, King Edward was preparing to return to Edinburgh for resupply. Just then he received information that the main Scottish army was encamped near the city of Falkirk. He immediately ordered a march, hoping to engage the Scots in a pitched battle in his favor - a battle he wanted desperately.

This battle occurred on July 22nd, 1298 and is the fated Battle of Falkirk. Seeing that Edward caught up with him and was ready for battle, William Wallace had no other choice but to fight the ill-fated battle. He was, however, outnumbered in every way: the Scots fielded some 5,000 infantry and 1,000 cavalry, while the

English fielded around 12,500 infantry and 2,500 cavalry. Even so, Wallace stood his ground. He resourcefully arranged his men into four great "schiltrons" - special formations akin to great square hedgehogs, bristling with spears. He further secured these schiltrons with sharp wooden stakes and ditches. However, he used them defensively, while his close advisor, Andrew Moray, used them offensively. The latter was not present, however, being mortally wounded at Stirling. This change of strategy might have been a contributing factor at Falkirk.

Early in the battle, the powerful English cavalry, split into two echelons, attacked the Scottish cavalry and archers. This clash was brief: the Scottish cavalry was quickly devastated and routed, and the archers dispersed. However, the English horsemen could not penetrate the dense forest of Scottish spears. Because of this, the English cavalry retreated, opening up the path for the English archers to arrive and deal with the fortified schiltrons. Here, the battle was effectively decided. The skilled Welsh archers, with their devastating longbows, had no trouble dealing with the Scottish spearmen. With no defenses and nowhere to hide, the spearmen in the schiltrons were devastated by arrow fire. Arrow after arrow claimed the lives of brave Scots who stood their ground, unable to act. When the schiltrons were thinned out and effectively broken, the English cavalry resumed its activity, charging at the devastated men and turning them on the run. The Battle of Falkirk was quickly over and was a devastating Scottish defeat. William Wallace was put to the challenge and could not deal with the overwhelming forces of the English. Historians long debated his skill as a military leader. Many say that he was exceptional in guerilla warfare and as a partisan leader but lacked the skills of conventional medieval warfare. Thus, when faced with a pitched open battle, he could not succeed. The historian Reid tells us that *"while unquestionably a good partisan leader, William Wallace's military abilities were simply not up to the job of organizing, training and leading a conventional military force. At Falkirk, Wallace simply drew up his army in an open field and froze."* After Falkirk, Wallace's military reputation was - sadly - shattered.

It was the sad truth that many somehow anticipated: the exceptional guerilla leader simply could not match an organized, professional army that was up to the standards of the day. Just a few months after this defeat, by September 1298 AD, William Wallace decided to resign from his position as Guardian of Scotland. He did so in favor of a new rising Scottish heroes: Robert the Bruce, Earl of Carrick, and John Comyn of Badenoch, the brother-in-law of the recent King John Balliol. Perhaps the main reason for this was the sudden lack of support and commitment from the lead Scottish nobles. Of course, the defeat at Falkirk further urged him to abandon his position. However, the dual-Guardianship assumed by Bruce and Comyn was a terrible mistake: the two men were bitter rivals in constant feud, and that meant that Scotland was ever nearer to a civil war, without a singular leader. Only after Comyn's murder, and the rise of Robert the Bruce, would Scotland gain a new capable leader who could finally lead it towards the shining bright lights of freedom.

Still, Wallace remained a vocal pursuer of total war with the English, and spurned attempts at peace. Sadly, after his defeat at Falkirk, history loses track of William Wallace. His movements and actions are vague at best, and he seems to have gone into hiding, or abroad. Some surviving evidence suggest that Wallace traveled as an envoy to the court of King Phillip IV of France, pleading for French assistance against the English. A letter survives, written by the French King, and dated to November 7th, 1300, AD, which is addressed to his envoys in Rome. The letter urges them to lend aid to Wallace in whatever way possible. This tells us that Wallace's diplomatic skills could have been satisfactory. We do not know if he traveled directly to Rome, perhaps in order to seek Papal aid, but it could be possible. Wallace's presence in France is quite certain: contemporary reports by English spies confirm his presence there.

By 1304, Wallace was back in Scotland, and his presence there seemingly noted by the English. Quite soon after he arrived in his home country, Wallace had to evade capture by the English, who wanted nothing more than to take hold of their bitter enemy. On February 20th, 1304, Sir William Wallace and Sir Simon Fraser, two major Scottish freedom fighters, were involved in the minor Battle of Happrew. Pursued by English nobles Robert de Clifford, John Segrave, and William de Latimer, as well as (at the time) English ally Robert the Bruce, Wallace and Fraser were forced to confront them at Happrew near Peebles. The patriots could not have numbered more than 500 men. Sadly, not much is known about the battle, except that it was a total English victory. Wallace and Fraser both escaped, and continued their run, being painted as rebels. Next, we hear of him is September 1304, when William Wallace is reportedly involved in the last major action of his life. It is the enigmatic Battle of Earnside, about almost nothing is known - not even its outcome. We only know that Wallace survived the battle and continued evading the English.

Alas, he could not evade them for long. William Wallace was captured on August 5th, 1305, at Robroyston near Glasgow, by a Scottish knight loyal to the English - Sir John de Menteith. Accounts tell us that Wallace was possibly captured treacherously: when he was in bed. It is possible that Menteith simply betrayed Wallace, and reported his presence to English soldiers, who came and captured him unexpectedly. Either way, the freedom fight of Scotland's great hero was now definitely finished. Almost immediately after capture, Wallace was transported to London, where he was initially lodged in the home of William de Leyrer, before being taken to the Westminster Hall. There, he was quickly put on trial. The English authorities crowned him with a garland of oak, which traditionally symbolized a king of outlaws. The trial declared him as a traitor and a war criminal, having committed atrocities against civilians, "sparing neither age nor sex, monk or nun". When declared a traitor, William Wallace coolly replied: "I could not be a traitor to Edward, for I was never his subject." Either way, in what was a certainty, William Wallace was declared guilty within minutes.

After the trial, on August 23rd, 1305, Scotland's great hero was led to meet his gruesome fate. Taken out from the Tower of London, Wallace was stripped naked, tied to a horse, and dragged thus through the city streets, all the way to the Elms at Smithfield, the place of the execution. This initial ordeal likely left him battered and scratched. Sadly, William Wallace bore the brunt of the English hate, and his death was nothing short of horrific. The penalty he was to suffer was to be hanged, drawn, and quartered - the traditional execution for traitors at the time. At the hands of the executioner, Wallace was strangled by hanging, but released while he was still alive. Then he was emasculated (his privates cut off); eviscerated (his bowels taken out and burned before his eyes); and then beheaded. Lastly, his body was dismembered into four parts. The English dipped his head into tar as to preserve it, then placed it atop a pike on London Bridge. The head of his brother John was also placed beside his at a later date, as well as the head of his co-fighter Simon Fraser, who was also drawn and quartered in 1306. Wallaces quarters (four parts of his body), were displayed in major towns: Berwick, Newcastle, Perth, and Stirling.

Thus ended one of Scotland's greatest heroes, William Wallace. His life was finished - but he continued to live for centuries after. His deeds won him immortality. Fighting only for Scotland and its cause, Wallace died as a martyr, and a hero of the people. Immediately after his demise, however, his death and sacrifice were honored only by a small band of faithful followers. The English King Edward thought himself rid of Scotland's foremost patriot, and thus thought that this nation was pacified. However, he was very much mistaken, for not only did he stir the Scottish spirits, but he also created an even greater enemy: Robert the Bruce. Finally understanding where his loyalties and ambitions lay, Robert the Bruce was ready to risk everything: his fortune, his nation, his titles, and his family name. He at last threw away the English yoke and embarked on a path that would lead Scotland to its much-coveted freedom, and Robert the Bruce to Kingship. Then, as if karma sought to at least cushion Wallace's death, it arranged that King Edward would not long outlive Wallace: he died in 1307.

It took Robert the Bruce eight long years of struggle and efficient guerilla warfare to finally lead Scotland to its independence. He struck a decisive victory in the Battle of Bannockburn, and thus avenged the death of William Wallace and all other Scottish men and women who fell in their struggle for freedom. It was Wallace who lit the flame of patriotism in the oppressed Scottish hearts: it was he who showed them that the English war machine *can* be fought, and that it *can* be stopped in its tracks.

Conclusion

Generations have written of William Wallace, inspired and moved to great deeds. It was as if this humble man gave his life in order to move an entire nation and tell them that greatness can be achieved - no matter what. However, it was only decades after his gruesome death that his sacrifice was recognized fully, for what it was. Once the Scottish nation understood what this great son of its people did, how badly he suffered for them all, that's when they hailed William Wallace as one of the greatest heroes that Scotland ever borne. Myths, legends, and tales were created, poems and books written, monuments erected and lofty memorials. Everything was done to perpetuate the sacrifice of Wallace for generations to come. Great poets and novelists of the world found inspiration in this man. Wordsworth, who was moved passionately by Wallace, wrote:

"IIuw Wallace fought for Scotland; left the name Of 'Wallace' to be found like a wildflower All over his dear country; left the deeds Of Wallace, like a family of ghosts, To people the steep rocks and riverbanks, Her national sanctuaries, with a local soul Of independence and stern liberty."

Still, it would not be right to look at William Wallace as a flawless man, perfect and uncorrupted. This is simply not the truth. No man ever to wield a sword in battle was a pure and sinless patriot. William Wallace was a man of his time, with the full meaning of that. He was a grizzled war commander, pursuing vengeance as much as he pursued freedom. He led raids into England, exacting vengeance on undeserving common folk. In the end - his ultimate motive was the freedom of his people and his nation. That is something we must always end at. Sadly, history does not remember much about Wallace

- many crucial details about his life and deeds are simply unknown to us. Poor chronicles and lack of writings leave much to be desired. What kind of a man Wallace was? What kind of character? What other deeds did he achieve? We simply may never know. Especially lacking is the period of several years after his defeat at the Battle of Falkirk. What happened at that time could have been full of deeds and adventures, now lost to us. In the end, we can only stick to what is known to us. That is a life of struggle for a man whose only ambition was the freedom of his nation. A younger son who devoted his life to war and a fight for independence - a common man who died young and in a terribly, blood-chilling manner. Whenever we retell the story of William Wallace, we are given a stark reminder of just how expensive freedom can be. Because of that, we owe a lot to William Wallace and all of the men like him.

References:

Alvarez, S. 2014. *William Wallace's Invasion of Northern England in 1297.* De Re Militari.

Brewer, R. 2010. *The Legend and Legacy of Sir William Wallace, Warrior, Martyr, and National Icon.* Legacy.

Campbell, R. *Sir William Wallace.* Unknown.

Donaldson, P. 1854. *The Life of Sir William Wallace: The Governor General of Scotland.* Andrus and son.

Fisher, A. 2012. *William Wallace.* Birlinn Limited.

Morton, G. 2014. *William Wallace.* Edinburgh University Press.

Murison, A. F. 2020. *Sir William Wallace.* BoD - Books on Demand.

Murison, A. F. 2012. *William Wallace: Guardian of Scotland.* Courier Corporation.

Ries, E. G. *The True History of William Wallace.* Electric Scotland.

Ross, D. R. 1999. *On the Trail of William Wallace.* Dundurn.

Don't miss out!

Visit the website below and you can sign up to receive emails whenever History Nerds publishes a new book. There's no charge and no obligation.

https://books2read.com/r/B-A-ODOK-TXLZB

BOOKS2READ

Connecting independent readers to independent writers.

Also by History Nerds

Ancient Empires
The Ottoman Empire
Rome: The Rise and Fall
The Mongol Empire
The Assyrian Empire
Ancient Egypt

Celtic Heroes and Legends
Celtic History
William Butler Yeats: Nobel Prize Winning Poet
Robert the Bruce
Scáthach
Finn McCool
William Wallace: Scotland's Great Freedom Fighter

Frauen des Krieges
Boudica: Königin der Icener
Jeanne d'Arc

Irena Sendler - Deutsche Ausgabe
Virginia Hall
Königin Amanirenas
Anne Frank
Florence Nightingale
Nakano Takeko
Lyudmila Pawlitschenko
Lagertha

Geschichte der welt
Die Geschichte Schottlands
Die Geschichte von Wales

Great Wars of the World
War Omnibus
World War 1
World War 2
The Napoleonic Wars: One Shot at Glory
The Serbian Revolution: 1804-1835
Peace Won by the Saber: The Crimean War, 1853-1856
The American Civil War

Pirate Chronicles
Grace O'Malley: The Pirate Queen of Ireland
Blackbeard
William Kidd

Ching Shih
Anne Bonny

The History of England
Roman Britain
Medieval England
The Wars of the Roses
Tudor England

The History of the Vikings
The History of the Vikings
Vikings
Longships on Restless Seas

Weltenbrand: Die großen Konflikte
Erster Weltkrieg
Zweiter Weltkrieg
Die Napoleonischen Kriege

Women of War
Women of War Omnibus: Books 1-10
Boudica: Queen of the Iceni
Joan of Arc
Irena Sendler

Virginia Hall
Queen Amanirenas
Anne Frank
Florence Nightingale
Nakano Takeko
Lyudmila Pavlichenko
Lagertha

World History
The History of the United Kingdom
The History of Ireland
The History of America
The History of Scotland
The History of Wales
The History of India
The History of Canada

Standalone
Grace O'Malley: Die Piratenkönigin von Irland

www.ingramcontent.com/pod-product-compliance
Lightning Source LLC
Chambersburg PA
CBHW031131160726

47989CB00017B/2879